HIP-HOP

Earl Simmons has come a long way from a troubled childhood to become DMX—hip-hop icon. The path wasn't always smooth, but he's proved that success can come from pain.

Hip-Hop

DMX

Toby G. Hamilton

Mason Crest Publishers

DMX

Produced by Harding House Publishing Service, Inc.
201 Harding Avenue, Vestal, NY 13850.

MASON CREST PUBLISHERS INC.
370 Reed Road
Broomall, Pennsylvania 19008
(866)MCP-BOOK (toll free)
www.masoncrest.com

Printed in the United States of America

First Printing

9 8 7 6 5 4 3 2 1

Library of Congress Cataloging-in-Publication Data

Hamilton, Toby G.
  DMX / Toby G. Hamilton.
      p. cm. — (Hip-hop)
  Includes index.
  ISBN 978-1-4222-0289-0
  ISBN: 978-1-4222-0077-3 (series)
  1. D M X—Juvenile literature. 2. Rap musicians—United States—Biography—
Juvenile literature. I. Title. II. Title: D M X.
ML3930.D2H36 2008
782.421649092—dc22
[B]
                              2007030444

Publisher's notes:
• All quotations in this book come from original sources and contain the spell-ing and grammatical inconsistencies of the original text.

• The Web sites mentioned in this book were active at the time of publica-tion. The publisher is not responsible for Web sites that have changed their addresses or discontinued operation since the date of publication. The publisher will review and update the Web site addresses each time the book is reprinted.

DISCLAIMER: The following story has been thoroughly researched, and to the best of our knowledge, represents a true story. While every possible effort has been made to ensure accuracy, the publisher will not assume liability for damages caused by inaccuracies in the data, and makes no warranty on the accuracy of the information contained herein. This story has not been authorized nor endorsed by DMX.

Contents

Hip-Hop Time Line

1970s DJ Kool Herc pioneers the use of breaks, isolations, and repeats using two turn-tables.

1976 Grandmaster Flash and the Furious Five emerge as one of the first battlers and freestylers.

1984 The track "Roxanne Roxanne" sparks the first diss war.

1988 Hip-hop record sales reach 100 million annually.

1982 Afrika Bambaataa tours Europe in another hip-hop first.

1970s Grafitti artist Vic begins tagging on New York subways.

1980 Rapper Kurtis Blow sells a million records and makes the first nationwide TV appearance for a hip-hop artist.

1985 The film *Krush Groove*, about the rise of Def Jam Records, is released.

1970   1980

1970s The central elements of the hip-hop culture begin to emerge in the Bronx, New York City.

1983 Ice-T releases his first singles, marking the earliest examples of gangsta rap.

1986 Run DMC cover Aerosmith's "Walk this Way" and appear on the cover of *Rolling Stone*.

1979 "Rapper's Delight," by The Sugarhill Gang, goes gold.

1974 Afrika Bambaataa organizes the Universal Zulu Nation.

1984 *Graffitti Rock*, the first hip-hop television program, premieres.

1988 MTV premieres *Yo! MTV Raps*.

1981 Grandmaster Flash and the Furious Five release *Adventures on the Wheels of Steel*.

1989 *Billboard* recognizes rap music as a category.

1993 Snoop Dogg's debut album *Doggystyle* becomes the first hip-hop album to debut at #1.

2003 50 Cent debuts with *Get Rich or Die Tryin.*

2006 The Smithsonian National Museum of American History announces the creation of a new hip-hop exhibition, scheduled to open in two years.

1997 The Notorious B.I.G. is gunned down in Los Angeles.

1990s Hip-hop gains popularity in Europe.

2004 The first National Hip-Hop Political Convention is held in New Jersey.

2007 Grandmaster Flash and the Furious Five are the first rap artists to be inducted into the Rock and Roll Hall of Fame.

1994 Nas releases *Illmatic,* which becomes the first album to ever receive a five out of five rating from *The Source.*

1990

2000

1994 In Puerto Rico, the musical genre that had been called "Dem Bow" or "Underground" now starts to be referred to as "Reggaeton."

2004 Daddy Yankee's single "Gasolina" rockets into mainstream popularity in the US, marking the rise of reggaeton in the US.

1990 In Puerto Rico, DJs inspired by Panamanian reggae begin to produce their own music.

1996 Tupac Shakur is killed in Las Vegas.

2003 For the first time, the top ten artists on the *Billboard* charts are all African American. Notably, they are all part of the Dirty South.

1992 DJ Playero releases his mixtape *32,* which has some of the earliest examples of reggaeton recorded, including a track by Daddy Yankee.

2001 Russell Simmons founds the Hip-hop Action Network.

2007 Numerous hip-hop artists perform at the Live Earth concerts, which take place around the globe.

If hip-hop is the music of the streets, of the real world, DMX knows of what he raps. He's lived the life he rhymes about, warts and all. But he also proves that if you want something badly enough, and are willing to work hard, it can be yours.

From the Streets: A Hip-Hop History

When it comes to sad stories, not many start out sadder than his. Earl Simmons was born in the projects to a single, teenage mom. He suffered a childhood of poverty and abuse. He ended up in group homes when he was just a kid. By the time he was a teen, he had a long record of run-ins with the law and his life was officially out of control. Emotional disturbance, drugs, crime, and violence took Earl into some of the darkest places a human spirit can travel. Many people don't return from that journey alive. If they do, they are alive only in body. Their minds and spirits are dead, murdered by the things they have seen and done. But Earl, who was already born with three strikes against him, refused to be taken out of the game. He fought his circumstances and his demons and became DMX—one of the biggest hip-hop stars in history.

The Real Deal

Today Earl Simmons is DMX, the multi-*platinum*-selling rapper. Since his big break in 1998, DMX has sold more than 20 million albums. He's credited with bringing the street back to hip-hop music, and hip-hop music back to the street. Never one to sell out or become a pop star, DMX is one of the most hardcore rappers around. He is an *icon* who came from the hood and became a prophet for his people. With his deep, gravelly voice, he raps about good and evil, life and death, God and the devil. He revels in destruction, and he sends up prayers for redemption. He is raw and emotional, and he calls himself a messenger of truth.

At first, record-industry executives refused to give DMX a chance. For years they claimed his music would never sell and his background would be a liability. When they looked at DMX, they saw a bitter, unpredictable, and out of control young man. They said DMX, with his street sensibilities, criminal background, hotheadedness, profanity-laced lyrics, and hardcore songs, would never appeal to the public. But they were wrong.

When the music industry finally gave DMX a chance, fans looked at the rap star and saw a real person bearing his soul. They saw a person who faced adversity and fought for survival by whatever means necessary. They saw a man who was unapologetic about his past but who wanted a better future. They saw a rapper who came from real-world struggles they could relate to, and they loved him. Hardcore rap fans didn't want a studio artist covered in bling. They wanted the real deal—a guy from the hood who had lived the life and fought the fight. DMX was their man.

DMX was more than a simple underdog. He was a dog that had been kicked, beaten, and caged again and again. But instead of giving up, whimpering and cowering in a corner, waiting for the meager scraps that would keep him alive, he came up fighting. Every time this dog got beaten down, he battled back lunging, growling, snapping, and biting. No matter the consequences, he refused to be tamed. His behavior scared a lot of people, and landed him in trouble with the law, but it also won him packs of fans.

It makes sense that hip-hop fans would fall in love with an artist like DMX. Like Earl Simmons, hip-hop was born in

The later decades of the twentieth century found many U.S. cities suffering severe problems. Some cities, like New York City, were experiencing white flight. People who could afford to do so (and they were mostly white), moved from the city to the suburbs. Low-income people of color became the primary residents of the inner cities.

the ghetto. From its earliest days, hip-hop music was about struggle, power, respect, and rising above difficult circumstances. It started as party music, but it quickly morphed into the angry shouts of frustrated youth. This music was born in the inner city and reflected the struggles and strife of the ghetto. For years it would be seen as urban or "street" music. It would also be considered "black" music, since in its early days the largest portion of its artists and fans were black. But calling hip-hop street or black music is far too simple. It is the music of disadvantaged, underprivileged, urban America, and to truly understand hip-hop's beginnings, you have to understand the history of the world into which it was born.

America's Crumbling Cities

Hip-hop music began in the 1970s, a turbulent decade in American history. The Vietnam War raged. An oil embargo starved the nation of fuel and crippled the economy. The Watergate scandal rocked Americans' faith in their politicians and led to President Richard Nixon's resignation. Racial tensions caused frustration, suspicion, and unrest. Anyway you looked at it, the 1970s held a lot of disruption and uncertainty for Americans.

Much of that disruption and uncertainty was concentrated in cities. By the time the seventies rolled around, "white flight" and urban decay had left America's metropolitan areas seething with poverty, crime, and unrest. The changes causing the urban turmoil had been under way for decades. During World War II (1939–1945), many people, including many black people, poured into the cities looking for work. After the war ended, however, major highway projects began all over the country. As interstates and freeways exploded, allowing people to travel farther faster, the flow to America's cities reversed. Now people left the downtowns behind for the space and manicured lawns of the suburbs. White flight occurred as working- and middle-class white populations left the cities.

As white and wealthier families left the downtowns, the businesses that serviced them followed, leaving storefronts abandoned and buildings vacant. Shopping malls and strip malls developed around the suburbs, and people needed the cities less and less. The hustle and bustle of many downtowns died away. Property values suffered. Tax revenue decreased, resulting in less money for inner-city schools and infrastructure, and neighborhoods went into decline.

Many people weren't bothered by the steady collapse of metropolitan areas. They were living the new American dream of suburban bliss. The troubles of the city seemed far away. But this new American dream, complete with its picket fences and tree-lined streets, wasn't open to everyone. In particular, black people were often left behind in the crumbling inner cities. Many black people simply didn't have the money to live in the suburbs. Others were prevented by racist economic practices, such as banks denying mortgages and loans to black customers. And then those few black people who could afford to move to the suburbs were often driven out by intimidation and violence. Slavery had ended with the Civil War, but racism and discrimination were still alive and well in America.

Inner Cities Seething with Anger

By the 1960s, many formerly vibrant and **diverse** urban neighborhoods had only poor populations. Some of these neighborhoods became sites for new, experimental forms of social housing. Old neighborhoods were leveled, and new ones, with low-rise and high-rise buildings catering to people with low incomes, were constructed. The plan was to provide decent, affordable housing to the urban poor. The reality,

Many people saw the discrimination that was occurring and were not content to sit by and let it continue. One of those individuals was the Reverend Dr. Martin Luther King Jr. His leadership helped change the world for everyone.

however, was concentrated areas of poverty and crime. People gave these neighborhoods the infamous name "the projects."

The poor, largely black populations trapped in the crumbling neighborhoods and crime-ridden projects seethed with anger. The transformation of inner cities was just one more example of how black people were still denied dignity, opportunity, and equality in America . . . and many people decided they weren't going to take it anymore. In the fifties and sixties, America's black people began to organize and demand recognition and rights. The civil rights movement developed. Black communities, under the leadership of people like W. E. B. DuBois and Dr. Martin Luther King Jr. organized bus boycotts, sit-ins, and marches. They made some great strides, like the abolishment of the "Jim Crow" laws that required and enforced segregation.

But the movement also met great resistance, and leaders were murdered. In response, black America's anger and frustration swelled. In 1965, civil rights and black empowerment leader Malcolm X was killed in a hailstorm of assassin's bullets. In 1968, Dr. Martin Luther King Jr. was shot and killed. The hopes and dreams of many black Americans died with him, and race riots exploded in many cities across the nation. As the sixties came to a close and the seventies began, the Black Power movement, led by organizations like the Nation of Islam and the Black Panther Party, took hold. Black and other minority populations in the inner cities had long struggled with poverty, racism, and frustration. Now those feelings mixed with a desire to rebel, rise up, become empowered, and demand recognition. Soon all these conditions and feelings would find expression in hip-hop music.

The Bronx: Where It Began

Hip-hop began in the Bronx, a borough of New York City. Like many urban neighborhoods, Bronx neighborhoods suffered from poverty, crime, and urban decay. In the 1950s, the

Cross-Bronx Expressway was built straight across the borough, destroying the neighborhoods in its path. In the sixties, housing projects sprang up, especially on the borough's south side. By the seventies, the Bronx's once-diverse neighborhoods were made up largely of poor black and Latino communities. The young people of these communities (like all young people) wanted to have fun. They also wanted recognition and respect. A new form of art and culture, called hip-hop, would allow them to have both.

Throughout human history, art has been something people use to express themselves and rise above their circumstances. Music, dance, painting, sculpture, poetry, prose, and theater are all forms of artistic expression that people use to enrich their own lives and communicate with others. All human cultures have forms of artistic expression. For black American culture, music has historically been especially important. From the spirituals sung in the era of slavery to the **R&B** of today, music has been a form of expression and salvation for black culture.

In the black and Latino communities of the Bronx in the 1970s, *funk*, disco, and soul were the popular music of the era. Music and dance parties were a great way for people to forget their troubles for a little while. Mobile DJs roamed, setting up their sound equipment for club parties, house parties, block parties, even parties in the parks. Out on the block or in a park, they had no electricity to power their sound systems, so they hotwired streetlights for juice. Often these parties weren't exactly legal (you were supposed to get a permit to have a party in public space, and hotwiring a streetlight was technically stealing electricity). But these parties also tended to be in rough neighborhoods. Local law enforcement often looked the other way, or even avoided the worst neighborhoods.

One of the most popular Bronx DJs was a Jamaican DJ called Kool Herc. He's often given credit for creating hip-hop

Down through the years, Latino and African American kids have loved music. They've used music to express themselves, to gain a sense of pride and achievement, and to just have fun. It was out of this atmosphere of creativity and culture that hip-hop first grew.

music by introducing two Jamaican styles to his shows. The first was cutting and mixing. The second was toasting. Cutting and mixing involved using two turntables, each with a record, and mixing back and forth between the two. This allowed a DJ to extend the breaks—the beat-driven, danceable portion of a song—as long as desired. Toasting was "shouting out" to the crowd. The DJ might toast by introducing himself (and any associates), telling jokes, boasting about his skills, or

DJs were king in the early days of hip-hop. They got their audiences up and dancing through their slick moves with two turntables and a mixer. Eventually, technology would take over many of their creative duties.

saying anything else to entertain the crowd during slow parts of a song or breaks in the music.

What DJ Kool Herc started, other DJs adopted, adapted, and perfected. Soon cutting and mixing was an art. DJs were taking **samples** and beats from songs and mixing them together, layering them, **scratching**, and adding all kinds of sound effects to create completely new musical compositions. Likewise, toasting evolved into a complex art form. At first it was just done by the DJs, but then emcees (MCs) took over, creating a style of speaking in rhythm and rhyme that they called rapping.

Hip-hop music began as dance music, but it quickly changed into something more. MCs started rapping about street life and its struggles. They began talking about the issues they saw all around them: poverty, racism, crime, drugs—in short, the harsh realities of their neighborhoods. Hip-hop became the voice of the black and Latino youth in the Bronx. It became a way for them to express their hopes, their dreams, their frustrations, and their rage. Hip-hop music was born.

Hip-hop was more than just music. It was an entire culture, including visual arts. In some communities, walls, subway cars, and almost anything else that stood still for a time became the canvases of graffiti artists. Some people see the images as an artistic representation of the world around them. Others just want them painted over.

Born into Lockdown

Soon a whole culture was developing around the new hip-hop music, and it involved dancing, art, fashion, and even language. One of the first hip-hop dance forms was b-boying—better known as break dancing. Break-dancers got down to DJ's beats with jaw-dropping moves. They mixed acrobatics and martial arts into their routines; they spun on their backs, shoulders, and heads; and they held difficult poses as shows of strength. Other urban dance styles, like pop-locking, which involved moving one's body in jointed, jerking rhythms, also contributed to the development of a hip-hop dance style.

Hip-hop art began with tagging, or graffiti. Taggers had names like Cornbread, Taki 183, and Case 2 that they scrawled on subway cars, bus shelters, bridges, and walls. Scrawling one's name on public structures may seem like simple vandalism, and sometimes it is. But over time some graffiti became art. Taggers adopted spray paint to "throw up" bigger and faster. They tried to outdo each other with size, color, complexity, and style. Sometimes they worked alone, and sometimes they worked in crews. Graffiti became a way that people expressed themselves, announced their presence, and claimed space as their own. Before long, graffiti was a defining part of urban America, and graffiti styles have influenced and inspired other forms of art.

Something to Believe In

One of the things that attracted young people to hip-hop was that anyone, no matter how poor or discriminated against, could do it. You didn't need to be a great singer or have special musical training to rap. You just needed a flow and a rhyme. That alone wouldn't make you a great rapper or allow you to win any MC battles, but it allowed you to participate in the culture and give your thoughts a voice. You likewise didn't need any special dance training to be a b-boy (or b-girl). You just needed the strength and the guts to bust some moves. And you certainly didn't need any art lessons to be a tagger. You just needed a can of paint, a name, and the daring to throw up. Being a DJ was more difficult; turntables and other equipment were expensive. But even people without the money for sound systems could make hip-hop music through beat boxing. A beat boxer created driving beats and complex percussion sounds using nothing but his mouth, throat, voice, and hands.

In the beginning, no one dreamed of becoming rich and famous through hip-hop. They were just expressing themselves, earning the respect of their peers, and defying authority and a society that wanted to forget the ghetto's existence. For a lot of young kids in the hood, hip-hop culture was a salvation. Many people certainly argued that hanging out rapping, dancing, and painting graffiti all over public structures was mischief making and law breaking. But in many ways it was a constructive outlet for kids whose energy might otherwise go into drugs, crime, and gangbanging. Of course, just because a young person was into hip-hop, didn't mean he'd stay out of trouble. It was the poor inner city after all, and there weren't a lot of opportunities for young black and Latino kids. Nevertheless, hip-hop gave them a way to express themselves and something to believe in.

If anyone in the world needed something to believe in, it was a young black kid named Earl Simmons. He was born on December 18, 1970, and lived with his mother and older sister, Bonita, in the School Street projects of Yonkers, New York. When he was just a little child, hip-hop started in the Bronx. Within a decade, the **underground** music was popular in New York City and making its way to other cities throughout the nation. By the time Earl was a young teen, he was listening to hip-hop music in group homes and rapping about the many troubles in his life. Once Earl was in his twenties, hip-hop was some of the most popular music on earth, and he was on his way to becoming a superstar.

In some ways, Earl had a normal childhood. He loved to draw. He enjoyed playing with Matchbox cars. He could entertain himself for a whole afternoon by sending toy paratroopers, complete with homemade, plastic-bag parachutes, sailing out of the apartment window. But you barely needed to scratch the surface to see that Earl's life was deeply troubled.

A Painful Childhood

In his autobiography, *E.A.R.L.: The Autobiography of DMX*, written with Smokey D. Fontaine, Earl describes a life that was hard from day one. When he was born, his mother was only nineteen years old. She already had a two-year-old daughter

Few people can go through the type of childhood DMX experienced and emerge unscathed. DMX wasn't one of them. Still, he had one constant in his roller-coaster childhood—a love of music. It was music that pulled him out of a life of poverty and despair.

who she struggled to care for. She didn't really like Earl's father that much; they definitely wouldn't be getting married, and she wasn't sure how she'd care for two children. Earl's father was a struggling artist, so there wouldn't be any checks coming from him.

Poverty wasn't the only hardship in Earl's youth. He was also plagued with illness. He inherited asthma from his father, and asthma attacks landed him in the hospital on a regular basis. Sometimes he'd have to stay as long as a week. He became even more familiar with the hospital when a drunk driver ran a red light and hit Earl, sending him tumbling beneath a parked car. The little boy was lucky to survive, but it took him a several weeks to recover.

The poverty, health problems, and injury might have been bearable if Earl had been surrounded by love. Unfortunately, that too was lacking in Earl's young life. His earliest memories include brutal beatings at the hands of his mother and her boyfriends. It wasn't long before beatings were a way of life, and Earl began to withdraw emotionally. The one person he felt truly loved him was his grandmother (his father's mother).

In his autobiography, Earl wonders if everything in his life would have turned out differently if he'd just been permitted to live with his grandmother, or if his father had remained a part of his life. But that didn't happen. His grandmother and mother didn't get along. He was never able to spend as much time with his grandmother as he wanted, and when she tried to intervene on his behalf, she was told to mind her own business. Earl's father sometimes took Earl with him when he sold art on the street, but then he moved to Philadelphia and had another family. Earl didn't see him again until he was an adult.

There was one small joy, however, in Earl's young life. Sometimes there was music. In an interview for *Rolling Stone*,

DMX remembered that when music was playing, he felt happy:

> *"When it was music playin', it was 'cause people were over. It was usually durin' the holidays, and they were havin' a good time. I had to look out my room down the hall, but I could see people dancin' and hear the music. . . . It was, like, the only time I was happy as a kid."*

No Turning Back

By the time Earl entered elementary school, he'd already experienced more pain and trauma than many people experience in a lifetime. He was an exceptionally smart kid, but he was also exceptionally angry and filled with distrust. Not long into his school career, he became exceptionally bored as well. He didn't feel challenged by the work, and he didn't see a payoff for doing well. If you completed an assignment or test before everyone else, you just had to sit quietly waiting for others to finish. There was nothing exciting in that.

Before long, Earl was looking for ways to entertain himself and was acting out his frustrations. When he finished a test long before the rest of the class, he began throwing spitballs. When he got restless and tired of his classmates, he'd stab one with a pencil. When he was kept after school for punishment, he'd go through other kids' desks and steal their belongings. Soon he was the "problem kid" of the school.

The more Earl acted out, the more he was beaten at home and punished at school. And the more he was beaten and punished, the more meaningless it all became. Soon Earl saw punishment as just an unavoidable part of life. He figured no matter what he did, he'd get into trouble somehow, so he just stopped trying to live by the rules. He was poor, hungry, abused, and neglected. Now he cared more about survival and eking out any pleasure he could from life (usually through mischief) than about getting good grades or obeying rules.

By the time he was ten years old, Earl was in his first group home. His mother's abuse and his own misbehavior had finally persuaded the courts to intervene, and Earl was sent to Julia Dyckman Andrus Children's Home for eighteen months. The time at Andrus was supposed to be an opportunity for rehabilitation, but Earl got into trouble there as well. He and

DMX didn't let stints of confinement to juvenile institutions stop him from developing his skills as a rapper. He knew that someday, those skills could bring him success.

another student started a fire, and later he attacked that student in class. When the school decided Earl's behavior was unmanageable, they began keeping him in isolation. In his autobiography, Earl describes how the isolation affected him:

> *"I couldn't stand not being able to do or eat what I wanted, couldn't stand being locked in, alone, for so many hours with nothing to do. . . . I started feeling like a caged animal. I was trapped. There was nothing that I could do or say to get out of that office. I began to listen to my instincts and my anger started to explode. Not only did I stop [caring] about everyone and everything around me, I began to believe all the bad that was ever said about me—Earl is manipulative, Earl is a problem, Earl has made his bed hard—and I swore that I would have the last laugh."*

Things only got worse after Andrus. At home, Earl's mom didn't let Earl or his sisters play outside. Eventually Earl got fed up and started staying out on the streets and running away. His mother punished him by making him stay in his room for days, weeks, a month, and eventually a whole summer. Earl was only allowed to come out for food and water. In his room he became even more bored, angry, and emotionally withdrawn.

His One Love

The grounding and punishments clearly had no positive effect, and as soon as Earl had the chance, he was out of the house and on the streets again. Eventually, he spent more and more time on the streets, and his mother tried to keep him locked up less and less. It was out on the streets that he found one thing to care about, one bright spot in his otherwise tortured and loveless life.

Dogs. What wonderful creatures. For most of us, they are loving companions that brighten our lives. For others, like DMX, dogs and other animals may provide the only love, friendship, and loyalty that they have. DMX spent much of his youth finding and adopting dogs that didn't have a home.

Some people might have wondered if DMX would even make it through his childhood and teen years. He didn't have support at home, and his behavior resulted in spending time in various juvenile facilities. To the surprise of some, DMX not only made it through his youth, he became a huge success.

One day, while wandering the streets, he found a stray dog. The dog ran from him immediately, but Earl was intrigued. He followed the frightened animal for hours, eventually getting close enough to pet it and lead it around. Later that day, the dog was frightened off by some older kids in the neighborhood, but a passion was started in Earl.

From that day on, Earl made finding and adopting stray dogs his mission. At first he'd try to bring them home, but time and again his mother got rid of them. Then he figured out he could hide his dogs up on the roof. He regularly camped out on the roof with a dog he'd found on the street, and caring for the abused, neglected animals taught him something important. It taught him about loyalty and unconditional love. His dogs didn't judge him. They didn't care what he did or what rules he broke. If he was kind to them, fed them, and loved them, they loved him back.

Earl learned another important lesson from his dogs. Once he gained a dog's trust, it became a fiercely loyal companion. It would protect him and fight for him. Out on the street, he always felt safe with a dog by his side. When he had a canine companion, people gave him more respect. He was still just a kid, but people learned not to mess with "Crazy Earl."

So how does one go from being a frequent guest at group homes to one of the biggest names in the music industry? Well, it requires hard work and talent of course. But as DMX will tell you, he didn't do it on his own.

3

Dark Man X

Earl wasn't able to run the streets for long. When he was thirteen, he was enrolled in another group home, Children's Village School for Boys. That's where he tried rapping for the first time. It was the early eighties, and hip-hop music had made its way out of the Bronx and was spreading around the country. At Children's Village, when a song with a strong beat came on the radio, some of the kids would gather round and rap to the beat, making up rhymes on the fly. The kids who rapped the best got respect from everyone else, and Earl was intrigued.

DMX Is Born

On his visits home, Earl noticed that hip-hop was suddenly big there as well. Each time he returned to Yonkers, he saw that the streets were transforming: rap music boomed from radios, throw ups were everywhere, and b-boys gathered on the corners. Then Earl heard beat boxing for the first time, and he decided to try it himself. He started experimenting. Soon he was really good, and Earl caught the attention of a local rapper named Ready Ron. Ron invited Earl to hang with him. They performed on the streets, Ready Ron rhyming and Earl providing the beats. When Earl went back to Children's Village he went back with a new name. He called himself DMX after one of the early drum machines.

But beat boxing wasn't the only thing Earl learned on the streets of Yonkers. He also learned about crime and drugs. At fourteen, he committed his first robbery. Soon he was robbing, not just for the money, but for the high, the thrill. At fifteen, he unknowingly did his first hard drugs when he smoked a joint laced with crack cocaine. That was a high he'd also want more of. After being released from Children's Village, Earl spent a year running the streets and beat boxing, but also robbing (he even trained his dog to steal from people) and getting high. Then one day he walked into school with a gun strapped to his leg. Shortly after his sixteenth birthday, he was behind bars at McCormick Juvenile Institution.

Hip-hop music was even bigger at McCormick than it had been at Children's Village. Earl no longer went by his given name, a name he had never particularly liked anyway. He went by the name DMX, The Beat Box Enforcer. But he soon saw that MCing was where it was at. Beat boxing was cool, but it didn't get the same respect (or the attention of the girls) as rapping. At McCormick, Earl underwent a transformation from a beat boxer to an MC.

Becoming a Rapper

Earl had a lot of time to think at McCormick, and he had a lot of time to write. Earl had always loved reading. Reading allowed him to escape into a different world. Now he started to feel the same way about writing. He had felt like a caged animal for so long. He was frustrated and angry. His whole life he had felt as though no one ever listened to him. He was so mixed up inside, he had no idea how to even begin unraveling his troubles.

When Earl decided to write his first rap, he discovered that writing not only helped pass the time, it allowed him to express himself in a way he never could before. And as he expressed himself, he began to better understand his life and his emotions. Soon he was pouring out his thoughts and feelings

It came as a surprise to few when DMX graduated from juvenile group homes to maximum-security prisons. Soon, DMX began the revolving-door cycle between prison, life on the street, and a return to prison.

in rhyme. When his stint at McCormick was done, he was no longer DMX, The Beat Box Enforcer. He returned to Yonkers as the rapper DMX the Great.

Back on the streets, however, rapping was still second to Earl's other activities. Nobody even tried to make him go to school anymore. He got back to robbing right away, and then he got into something even worse: stealing cars. Stealing cars earned Earl his first stint in a maximum-security prison. It was again time to think, rap, and write. While in prison, he started battling other rappers, and when he won, he gained confidence in his skills. Soon rapping gave him a focus and purpose that he never had before. He cared about rapping more and getting into trouble less. But still, once he was back on the streets, it didn't take long for him to pick up his bad habits.

A New Love

As Earl's teenage years came to a close, he had a well-established cycle. Get into trouble. Spend some time in jail. Get out of jail. Get into trouble again. Go back to jail. But there was one positive development in his life. Her name was Tashera. Earl was in elementary school when he first saw a young Muslim girl wearing flowing blue and white robes. He never spoke to her, but throughout his childhood, he sometimes thought about her. For reasons he could never understand, her image stayed in his mind.

Imagine his surprise, then, when one evening at a club a friend introduced him to Tashera. It turned out Tashera had lived near Earl his entire life. More surprisingly, she had been that young Muslim girl wearing the robes. It didn't take long for Earl and Tashera to fall in love. In the coming years it would become clear that Tashera would stand by Earl no matter how much trouble he got into.

Tashera was one shining light in Earl's life and rap was the other. As Earl approached his twentieth birthday, rap became the focus of nearly all his energy. Everywhere he went, he looked for MCs to battle. He battled on the street, at parties, and in clubs. He battled in jail, around Yonkers, across the Bronx, and throughout Manhattan. Rap music had broken through to **mainstream** radio. Artists like Run-D.M.C., Ice-T, Public Enemy, the Beastie Boys, and 2 Live Crew were all becoming huge, and Earl began to believe that he too might have a future in the music industry.

Trying to Break In

In 1990, *Source* magazine named DMX "The Best Unsigned Rapper in the Country" in their column, "Unsigned Hype." It was a huge day for Earl, but it did nothing to keep him out of trouble or jail. A lifetime of abuse, drugs, crime, anger, frustration, and incarceration had taken a serious toll on Earl's psyche. In his autobiography, he describes his personality starting to pull apart into Earl (the person he once was), DMX (the rapper), and X (the caged animal who lived and breathed rage):

> *"See, DMX was the rapper. But X, X was someone different. X was hunger. X was rage. And when I found X locked up in that cell, I knew that I was losing Earl. X lived in a place within me that I knew a young boy could never survive. Almost like a monster. I could feel its force pulse through my veins. And when he showed himself, my music took on a whole new identity. I was still writing, but now my phrases were hostile and my stories were dark. Unconsciously, my words formed sentences that were loaded with the anger and frustration I carried with me every second of every day. I spit fire at anybody who came my way and slowly a new persona evolved out of the words of my own experience."*

X was angry and destructive, but he also wrote powerful lyrics. As time went by, Earl faded, and X grew. By the time he was twenty, Dark Man X (as he began calling himself) was sniffing around for his first record deal, but he was also struggling with drugs and what he describes in his autobiography as dark "episodes." During one of these episodes, he even stole a television from his manager. Soon, however, he realized he needed to fight the drugs and keep the darkness at bay. Tashera was pregnant, and as soon as Earl heard the news, he knew

When DMX's son was born, it was a wake-up call for the young musician wannabe. But it didn't keep him out of prison, at least at first. During one of his stays at a state-run "hotel," he was finally ready to reach out to someone. His uncle helped DMX find his spiritual side so he could be there for his son.

he wanted to be a father. Shortly before his twenty-second birthday, his son, Xavier, was born.

Not long after his son's birth, however, Earl was back in prison, this time in solitary confinement. And while there, someone finally got through to him and made him start looking for a higher purpose and power in his life. His Uncle Ray, one of his mother's younger brothers, set the change in motion. Ray was a social worker. He had only really met his nephew once before, but he decided to start visiting Earl in jail. In his autobiography, Earl says that for some reason, his Uncle Ray was able to get through to him when no one else could:

"[Ray] said he wasn't there to judge me, he just wanted to help, give me some tips on how to improve my situation and bring some light into my life. Over the years, I refused to listen to anyone that kicked it to me that way. X would bark at them and bite their hand off before anyone could even begin to speak of upliftment or purpose or light. But months in solitary confinement gave me nothing but time to think. There was a freedom and a comfort there that I had felt many times before. Being alone day after day in the dark and the quiet allowed my mind to take me places that I had never gone before and one cold night I just closed my eyes and reached out, reached for the sky."

This time in prison, something was different for Earl. This time, he started to pray. He started to write raps that were conversations with God. He started to search for light, guidance, and meaning in his suffering. He started to want to change.

With a new sense of spirituality—and a new family to support—DMX was ready to begin a life on the straight and narrow. But he quickly found out that was easier said than done. He tried traditional jobs, but things never seemed to work out for long. DMX knew what he wanted to do, and that was become a rapper—not a nine-to-fiver.

4

Dog's Day

When Earl got out of prison this time, he tried harder to stay out of trouble. He now had a family to support, and he tried to hold down a real job. The jobs never lasted long though, and he soon had a string of failed attempts at regular employment. But rapping was still what he wanted to do anyway. For a while now he had been signed with a start-up hip-hop production company called Ruff Ryders.

Broken Body . . .

Ruff Ryders had been signing artists and trying to get recording contracts for years with very little success. Now, finally, they were getting some artists onto the hip-hop map, but Earl wasn't one of them. He had a brief stint with Columbia Records, but when his debut single "Born Loser" failed to hit, he was "released from his contract," a kind way of basically saying "You're fired."

Wherever DMX performed, crowds went wild, but music executives weren't biting. They figured DMX was simply not a safe investment.

To Earl, it seemed like he'd been taking body blows his whole life. Now, while his musical career was going nowhere, two more big blows came. The first was the death of his grandmother. When Earl was a child, his grandmother was the only person in the world he felt really loved him. She was the only one he could trust. Her death was devastating. Then his beloved dog, Boomer, a fearless pit bull who Earl loved and trusted more than most people, was hit and killed by a car. Boomer wasn't just a dog; Boomer was Earl's kindred spirit and constant companion. As Earl stood helpless, watching Boomer die in the street, he felt some of the greatest pain he'd ever known.

Then Earl almost died. It went down over a gold chain and a jacket. A kid accused Earl of stealing them (this time Earl actually wasn't the thief), and the kid's father came with a group of guys looking for payback. Over the years, Earl had earned quite the reputation in Yonkers and made a lot of enemies. When the group of men started beating Earl in the street, no one came to help him. In fact, some even joined in on the beating. He was kicked mercilessly, dragged into a park, and narrowly avoided having his head smashed by a brick. He was left with a broken nose, a broken upper and lower jaw, and a swelling abscess on his throat. He had to have surgery to reset his bones, and he spent the next three months with his jaw wired shut.

◆ ◆ ◆ Fighting Spirit

Once again, Earl had a lot of time to think, and he began to think that perhaps he was reaping what he sowed. Maybe this was payback for all the times he'd taken advantage of other people. Perhaps God was trying to send him a message. At first he wanted to kill his assailants. But he decided to let the

Timing is everything. Or is it? Just as DMX decided to make a real go at becoming a rapper, he was attacked and his jaw was wired shut. But that didn't stop the determined young man. He rapped through the wires, and the music execs liked what they heard.

anger go instead. Then he decided that, mouth wired shut or not, he was going to rap. Straining, drooling, and in incredible pain, he began spitting out rhymes through his locked teeth. The words had a new commitment and *vengeance*. He was like a man possessed.

In this restrained, debilitated, yet fearsome state, Earl finally convinced someone to take a chance on DMX. Lyor Cohen, president of Def Jam Records, had heard DMX rapping on a *mixtape*. He wanted to hear more. Earl's Ruff Ryder associates urged him to wait until his jaw was healed. Earl refused. He was caged. He was exploding. He needed to be heard, *now*!

He went to the recording studio where Lyor Cohen and all of the Ruff Ryder crew waited. Years later, in an article by William Shaw for *Blender*, Lyor Cohen remembered what it was like as the other rappers stepped away to let DMX take the mic saying, "It was like cockroaches running away. . . . I felt like he levitated."

DMX stepped to the mic, and through his clamped jaws spat out "The Convo" with all the power and force of his soul. The rap was a conversation between him and God, and it was the purest, most honest thing he had ever written. When the prayer was over, he dove into "Let Me Fly," another raw, truthful rhyme that laid bare his soul. Lyor knew in an instant: DMX was the new face, heart, and soul of hip-hop.

Hip-Hop's New King

Earl Simmons had spent more than twelve years trying to become a rapper, banging his head against the music industry's doors, with no one answering. Then, instantaneously, he became Def Jam Records' hottest artist. It began in 1997, with guest appearances on singles by other Def Jam artists LL Cool J, Mase, and The LOX. Then, in 1998, DMX released his first single, "Get at Me Dog." The song introduced the world to DMX's deep, gritty voice, a voice *Rolling Stone* would later describe as, "the sound of gravel hitting the grave." It also had DMX growling and barking. When the song hit the streets, his popularity exploded.

Shortly after, DMX released his first full-length album, *It's Dark and Hell is Hot*. In his autobiography, he remembers all the uncertainty he felt as he prepared to bare his soul to the world in music. He didn't know if the world could accept what he had to say. He writes, "I just knew that I was trying my best to pour twenty-seven years of my life into the words of sixteen songs and a prayer."

The album debuted at #1 on the *Billboard* 200 album chart. It eventually sold more than five million copies worldwide and was certified quadruple platinum. It was a stunning debut for a hardcore hip-hop artist. But what happened next was even more impressive. In December, just seven months after releasing his first album, his second album, *Flesh of My Flesh, Blood of My Blood* hit store shelves. It too came out swinging, grabbing the #1 spot on the *Billboard* 200, selling a phenomenal 670,000 copies in the first week, and eventually going triple platinum. With that, DMX made history by becoming the only hip-hop artist (and only the second artist in *Billboard* history) to have two albums debut at #1 in the same year.

Earl's joy in the incredible success of that year, however, was slightly dampened when a woman accused him of rape. Once again he was dragged into court. This legal battle, however, had a happy ending for Earl. DNA evidence presented at trial showed he could not have been the woman's assailant and cleared his name. Earl was free to enjoy his new success as DMX.

A New Life

After a lifetime of poverty, hurt, anger, and struggle, opportunity was suddenly everywhere. DMX's musical success earned him his first offer of a film role. Suddenly DMX was on the big screen with fellow rappers Method Man and Nas in the movie *Belly*. Other movie roles quickly followed, including a costarring credit alongside Jet Li in *Romeo Must Die*, and starring with Steven Seagal in *Exit Wounds*—a film that, like DMX's albums, would debut at #1 at the box office.

Things were going great in his personal life as well. He and Tashera, the love of his life, the woman who had stood by him through all the hard times, got married. Earl had first seen

Few people meet their soul mates when they are children, but perhaps DMX and Tashera are the exceptions. For DMX, it might have even been love at first sight when he caught a glimpse of a young Tashera. When they met as young adults, Tashera proved her love for the troubled musician by sticking by him despite his problems.

Tashera as a child dressed in blue and white robes; now he rejoiced to see her walking down the aisle in a white wedding gown. He realized that, though life had been hard from the very beginning, though he had seemed cursed from the start, in Tashera's presence he had always been blessed.

DMX's incredible musical success also continued. In December 1999, a year after the release of *Flesh of My Flesh, Blood of My Blood*, DMX released his third album, . . . *And Then There Was X*. Once again, it debuted at #1 on the *Billboard* 200 chart, making him the only hip-hop artist to have his first three albums debut at #1. . . . *And Then There Was X* also became his best-selling album, eventually going six-times platinum. The Dog, as many people now called him, had arrived.

As the twentieth century came to a close, there were few hip-hop artists hotter than DMX—The Dog. It seemed as though everything he touched hit #1. It looked as though the new millennium would be even better.

5

No Regrets

In 2001, DMX continued his #1 streak with the release of his fourth album, *The Great Depression*. After debuting in the top spot on the *Billboard* chart, it went on to platinum sales. His fifth album, *Grand Champ*, came out in 2003. Again the album opened at the top spot on the *Billboard* chart, making DMX the only artist in history to have five albums debut at #1. It must have come as a shock, then, when fans heard DMX say he was retiring from the music business. He said he was turning away from music to spend more time with his family, be more involved in the church, and concentrate on his acting career.

In 2003, DMX again starred alongside Jet Li in a movie called *Cradle 2 the Grave*. In 2004, he played the role of King David, a drug lord, in the movie *Never Die Alone*. The movie was based on a novel by Donald Goines. DMX had read his first Goines novel while in jail and became a fan. When he heard that one of Goines's books was being turned into a movie, he jumped at the chance to be involved. In an interview, DMX talked about the new movie and how he was able to draw from his own life for the film:

> *"I had actual events and issues to draw from. I think that is the theme of my life. Right, wrong, good, bad, heaven, hell. I think you have to know both in order to honestly choose one. So I'm familiar with both sides of the fence. That was the character. All right, be a grimy [guy] for a minute, then [look] around and get a conscience."*

Coming Back

DMX's retirement from music, however, was short lived. For DMX fans, 2006 brought good news. After switching from Def Jam to Sony, DMX announced his plans to release his sixth studio album, *Year of the Dog . . . Again*. The record label change wasn't the only change in DMX's musical life, however. An article by Shaheem Reid, which came from a re-port on MTV News and appeared on vh1.com, stated that DMX was also thinking of changing his stage name. The article quotes DMX as saying that changing his stage name would be a spiritual move to bring better energy into his life:

> *"'It's just the whole Dark Man thing,' [DMX] continued. 'Because if you look at it, from a spiritual point of view, the Bible teaches us that we can speak things into existence. . . . And Dark Man, you know, it may not be the best name for me.'"*

Imagine fans' surprise when DMX announced he was retiring from the music scene. There were other, more important things that he wanted to spend time doing. DMX was on top, but he was willing to put performing, and his fame, aside.

The article went on to say that DMX was considering changing his name to Dog. So far, however, no such change has occurred. In August 2006, *Year of the Dog . . . Again* hit store shelves. It was DMX's first album to miss the #1 spot on the *Billboard* 200 album chart, debuting at #2 instead. It is also his first album that didn't achieve platinum sales.

The sales for *Year of the Dog . . . Again* may have been disappointing, but they couldn't change DMX's place in hip-hop history. DMX is now one of the most successful rappers in of

After a brief retirement (very brief), DMX was back on the music scene. The question was whether he would remain DMX. He talked about changing his stage name to something less spiritually negative. So far, he's been content to stick with DMX.

all time. He is a millionaire and a movie star. He is married to the love of his life, and together they now have three beautiful children. In 2007, he released a greatest hits/**compilation** album called *The Definition of X: The Pick of the Litter*. His next album, *The Resurrection of Hip-Hop* is expected out in 2008.

Still Tortured, Still Troubled

While DMX's career has soared, however, his troubles with the law have also continued. It seems, no matter how far Earl goes, bars are always somewhere close by. Since his explosion onto the hip-hop scene, he has been arrested and jailed on a number of occasions. Driving without a license, drug possession, and assault are just some of the charges against him in recent years.

At the end of the day, however, don't expect any apologies from DMX. He's lived the hard life. He's questioned the meaning of it all. He's earned fame and fortune. But he still struggles and lives on the edge. Every album he's put out contains at least one song that is a conversation with God or about DMX's quest to find God and meaning in his life. But then other songs are jaunts into a world of darkness, where X the thug comes out to howl and play. It seems DMX's songs are a reflection of his life. His real life is also, and perhaps always will be, filled with these same contradictions.

And so, what will happen to Earl in the future remains to be seen. As he pursues his career and seeks enlightenment, his demons travel with him, and they could yet overtake him. Today, despite all his success, he still slips into the dangerous behaviors of his past. He's open about this fact, and he feels no regrets. DMX would probably be the first to say that he's a rapper, not a role model. In his opinion, if you want to run with "the Dog," you have to be realistic about who he is: a guy from the 'hood who learned to survive by whatever means necessary.

Despite his continuing scuffles with the legal system, DMX remains an extremely successful rapper. He received a special award from *Billboard* for having his first four albums debut at the top spot on the charts.

In interviews and his music, DMX refers to his life as "a war." He says within him there is a constant battle between good and evil. Sometimes the good conquers. Sometimes the evil wins out. But he doesn't want people to write him off as a failure or hopeless case just because he still falls sometimes. Instead, he wants fans to realize that the war is still on. He's still fighting, and he doesn't want any decisions made until the final round is slugged out and the last bell rung. For DMX, for Earl Simmons, the jury is still out. Judgment day has yet to come.

1970s   Hip-hop begins in the Bronx section of New York City.

Dec. 18, 1970   Earl Simmons—DMX—is born.

1990   *Source* magazine names DMX "The Best Unsigned Rapper in the Country."

1997   DMX appears on singles by fellow Def Jam artists LL Cool J, Mase, and The LOX.

1998   DMX releases his first single.

DMX's first album debuts at #1 on *Billboard*'s 200 album chart.

Flesh of My Flesh, Blood of My Blood debuts at #1.

DMX is charged with rape, but is cleared.

DMX costars in his first film, *Belly*.

1999   . . . *And Then There Was X* debuts at #1 on the charts.

2000   DMX costars in *Romeo Must Die*.

2001   *The Great Depression* debuts at #1.

DMX receives a special award at the *Billboard* Music Awards for having his first four albums debut at #1.

DMX costars in *Exit Wounds*.

2003   *Grand Champ* debuts at #1.

DMX announces his retirement from the music business; he later changes his mind.

DMX costars in *Cradle 2 the Grave*.

2004   DMX costars in *Never Die Alone*.

2006   *Year of the Dog . . . Again* becomes DMX's first album not to debut at #1.

DMX contemplates changing his stage name.

2007   *The Definition of X: The Pick of the Litter* is released.

2008   *The Resurrection of Hip-Hop* is released.

Albums

1998	It's Dark and Hell Is Hot
1998	Flesh of My Flesh, Blood of My Blood
1999	. . . And Then There Was X
2001	The Great Depression
2003	Grand Champ
2006	Year of the Dog . . . Again
2007	The Definition of X: The Pick of the Litter
2008	The Resurrection of Hip-Hop

DVDs

2000	Backstage
2001	DMX—Angel
2001	Ruff Ryders: Uncensored
2001	The Best of DMX: Make It or Break It
2002	DMX on DVD
2004	DMX—The Dark Prince
2005	Smoke Out Festival Presents: DMX
2006	Ride or Die
2004	Never Die Alone

Films

1985   *Belly*

2000   *Romeo Must Die*

2001   *Exit Wounds*

2003   *Cradle 2 the Grave*

2004   *Never Die Alone*

Book

DMX and Smokey Fontaine. *E.A.R.L.: The Autobiography of DMX*. New York: Harper, 2003.

Awards/Recognitions

1999   American Music Awards: Favorite Male Artist, Rap/Hip-Hop; *Billboard* Music Awards: R&B Albums Artist of the Year.

2000   Soul Train Music Awards: Sammy Davis Jr. Entertainer of the Year Award, Male.

2001   *Billboard* Music Awards: Special award for First Four Albums Debuting at #1.

Books

Bogdanov, Vladimir, Chris Woodstra, Steven Thomas Erlewine, and John Bush (eds.). *All Music Guide to Hip-Hop: The Definitive Guide to Rap and Hip-Hop.* San Francisco, Calif.: Backbeat Books, 2003.

Chang, Jeff. *Can't Stop Won't Stop: A History of the Hip-Hop Generation.* New York: Picador, 2005.

DMX and Smokey Fontaine. *E.A.R.L.: The Autobiography of DMX.* New York: Harper, 2003.

Emcee Escher and Alex Rappaport. *The Rapper's Handbook: A Guide to Freestyling, Writing Rhymes, and Battling.* New York: Flocabulary Press, 2006.

George, Nelson. *Hip Hop America.* New York: Penguin, 2005.

Kusek, Dave, and Gerd Leonhard. *The Future of Music: Manifesto for the Digital Music Revolution.* Boston, Mass.: Berkley Press, 2005.

Light, Alan (ed.). *The Vibe History of Hip Hop.* New York: Three Rivers Press, 1999.

Waters, Rosa. *Hip-Hop: A Short History.* Broomall, Pa.: Mason Crest, 2007.

Watkins, S. Craig. *Hip Hop Matters: Politics, Pop Culture, and the Struggle for the Soul of a Movement.* Boston, Mass.: Beacon Press, 2006.

Web Sites

DMX Official Web Site
www.dmx-official.com

DMX in *Rolling Stone*
www.rollingstone.com/artists/dmx

DMX on MTV
www.mtv.com/music/artist/dmx/artist.jhtml

DMX on VH1
www.vh1.com/artists/az/dmx/artist.jhtml

Glossary

compilation—Something created by gathering things from other sources.

diverse—Very different or distinct from one another.

funk—A musical style that comes from jazz, the blues, and soul and is characterized by a heavy backbeat.

icon—Someone widely and uncritically admired as symbolizing a movement or field.

mainstream—The ideas, actions, and values that are most widely accepted by a group or society.

mixtape—A compilation of songs recorded from other sources.

platinum—A designation that a recording has sold one million units.

R&B—Rhythm and blues; a style of music developed by African American musicians that combines elements of jazz and the blues.

samples—Pieces of recorded music taken from an existing recording and used as part of a new recording.

scratching—Deliberately sliding the record needle across a record that is being played.

underground—Separate from the main social or artistic environment.

vengeance—Punishment that is given in return for a wrong.

Index

About the Author

Toby G. Hamilton was born in 1979 in Binghamton, NY. As an author and illustrator, Toby is interested in art's power as a tool of self-expression, social commentary, and political activism. Toby is especially interested in hip-hop's role in twenty-first century America and its increasing power as a revolutionary force around the world.

Picture Credits

Bielawski, Adam / PR Photos: pp. 2, 8, 43
iStockphoto: pp. 18,
   Dewis, Rachel: p. 11
   Leigh, Scott: p. 20
   Lerich, Robert: p. 17
   Migin, Melvin: p. 29
   Snow, Eliza: p. 35
   Young, Nicole S.: p. 46
Library of Congress: p. 14
PR Photos: front cover, pp. 24, 27, 30, 32, 40, 48, 51, 52, 54
Walck, Tom / PR Photos: p. 38

To the best knowledge of the publisher, all other images are in the public domain. If any image has been inadvertently uncredited, please notify Harding House Publishing Service, Vestal, New York 13850, so that rectification can be made for future printings.